BRAIN GAMES

PUZZLES TO KEEP YOUR MIND SHARP

AGE 3+

DREAMLAND PUBLICATIONS
J-128, Kirti Nagar, New Delhi -110 015, India
Tel : +91-11-2510 6050, 2543 5657
E-mail : dreamland@dreamlandpublications.com
Shop online at www.dreamlandpublications.com
Follow us www.instagram.com/dreamland.publications

Published 2026 by
DREAMLAND PUBLICATIONS
J-128, Kirti Nagar, New Delhi - 110 015, India
Tel : +91-11-2510 6050, 2543 5657
E-mail : dreamland@dreamlandpublications.com
www.dreamlandpublications.com

Printed in India

PREFACE

'Brain Games' Activity series is specially designed to cater to the young and creative minds of today's generation. This set of four books aim to develop the cognitive and analytical skills in children through an array of innovative activities. Each book includes mazes, dot to dot, match the things, spot the differences, colouring by code and many more. This series focuses on enhancing the children's intellect and promptness in problem-solving and motor skills. 'Brain Games' is a perfect series for children to develop their overall confidence and knowledge.

Farm time! Tick the animals that you see on a farm.

Rise and shine! Number the pictures in order of your morning routine.

Help John understand emotions. Match the faces showing various emotions with the correct names.

Happy | sad | confused | surprised

1 2 3 4

Let's join the dots! Start with number **1** and then connect all the dots till the end You will discover a picture of a cute animal.

Match the body parts with the correct clothing for them.

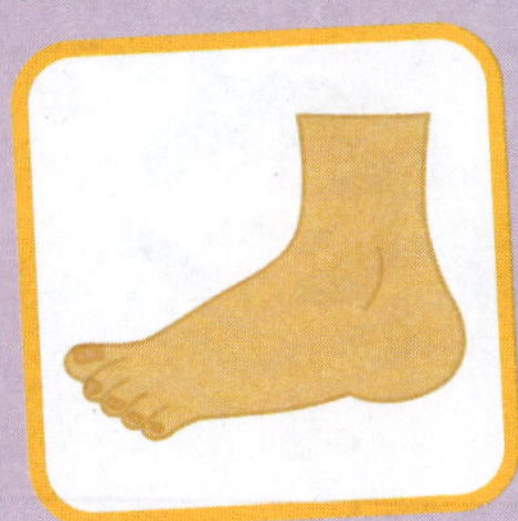

Which of these fruits are yellow in colour? Colour them in yellow here as well.

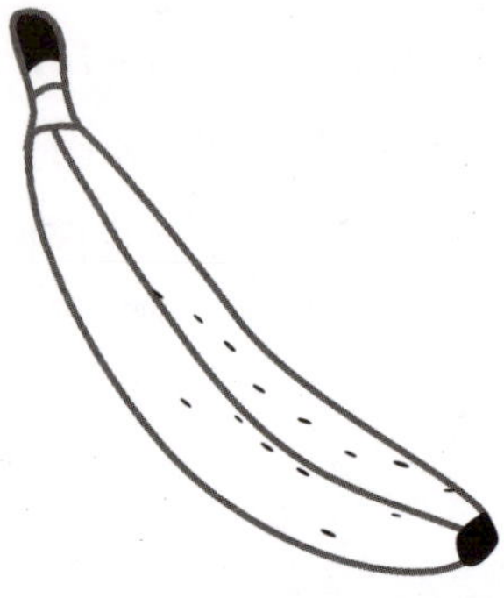

Help the caterpillar reach its mamma butterfly.

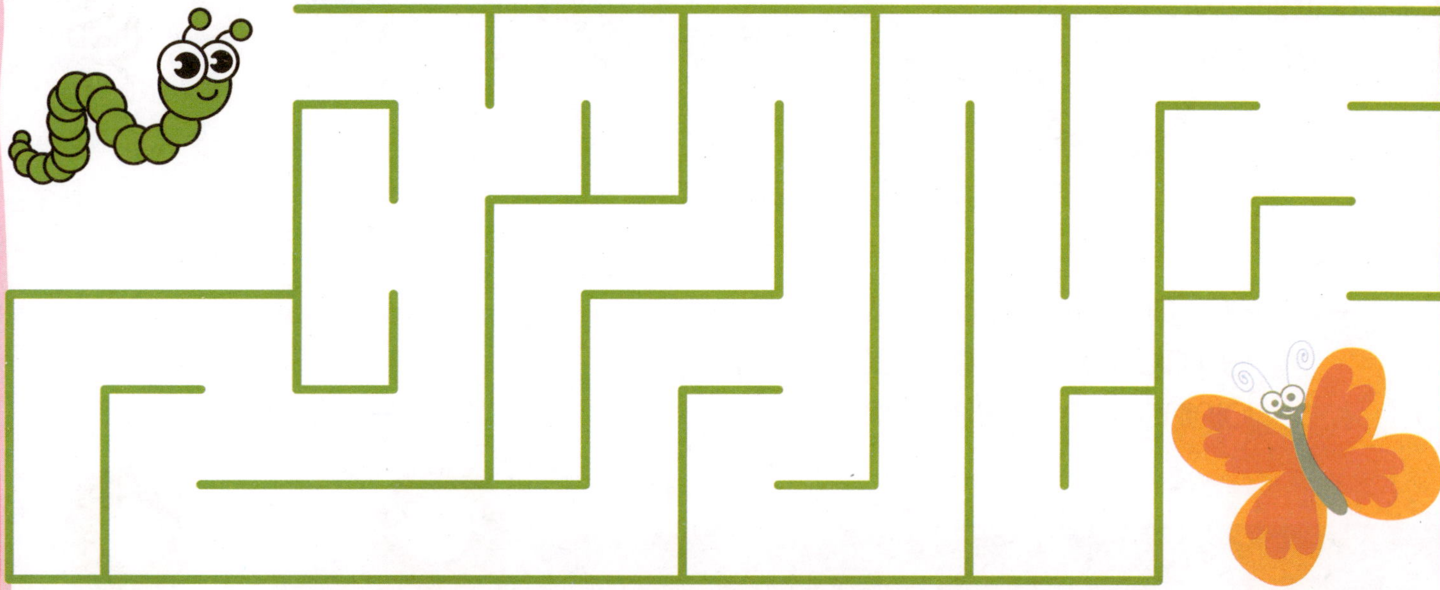

Look at the little ducklings walking in different directions. Tick the one showing its back.

Emma is sleeping. Can you spot the stars and circle them without waking her up?

Circle the two pictures that look alike.

Help the little bear drive in the middle of the road by joining the dashed lines.

Find and circle these animals in the big picture.

Quack! quack! Connect the dots to make a duck and then colour it.

Match each body part with the correct clothing.

1 2 3 4 5

A B C D E

Tick the odd one out.

Spot at least 5 differences.

Match the objects of space to their correct shadows.

Which of these fruits are red in colour? Colour them in red here also.

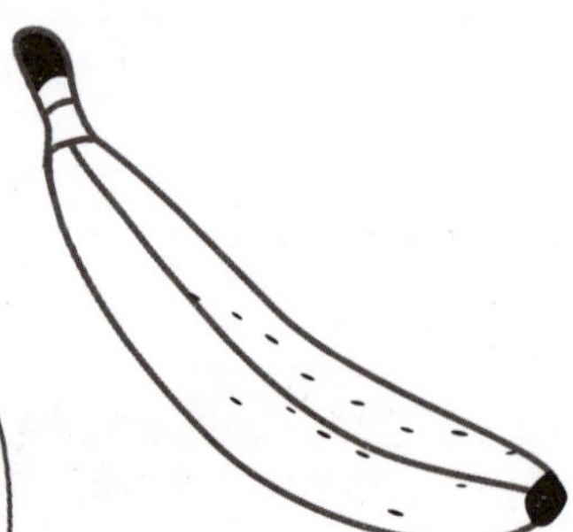

Help Liam find his pet dog.

Are the blue birds and yellow birds equal in number? Write Yes or No in the circle.

It's colouring time! Let's colour the picture according to the colour given for each number.

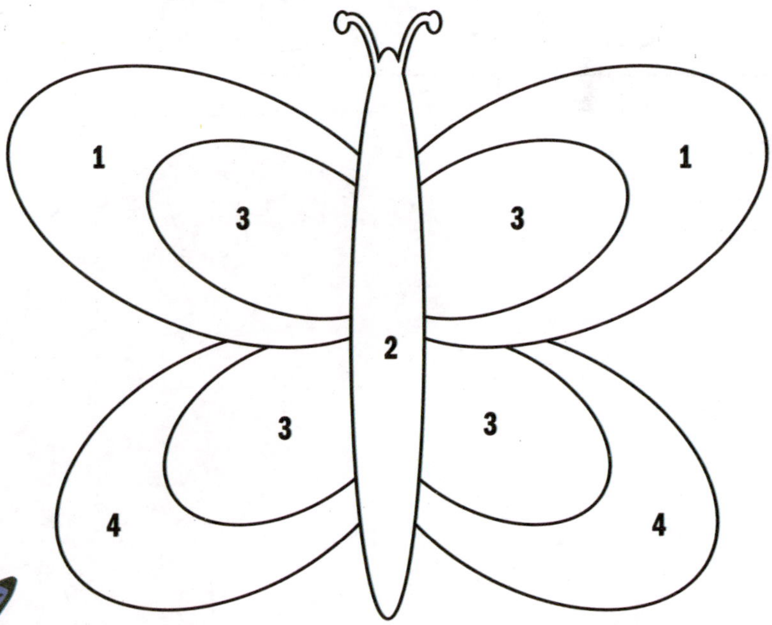

This is what Mia does every night.
Order the pictures correctly by writing 1, 2, and 3 under them.

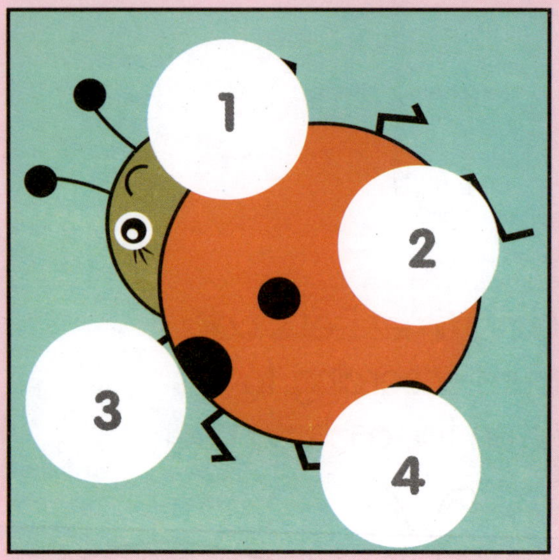

Draw lines to place each piece in the correct circle and complete the picture.

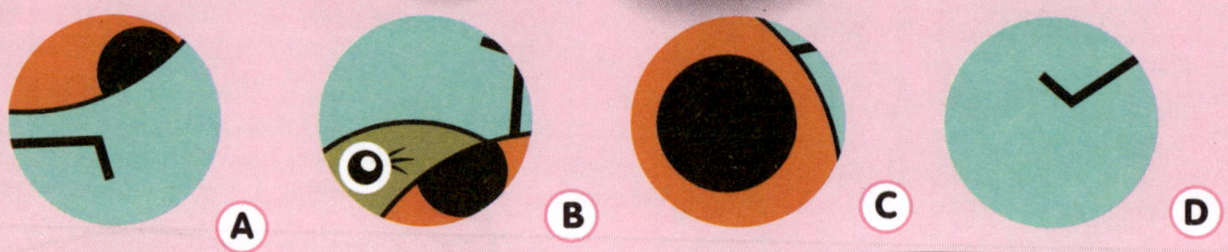

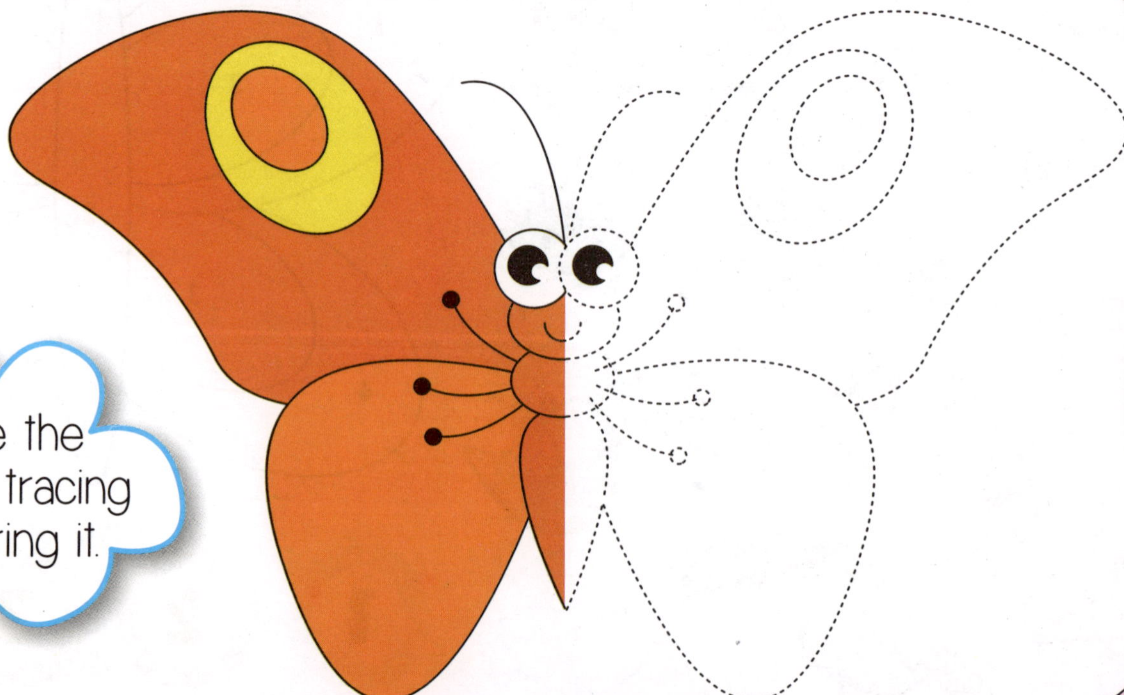

Complete the butterfly by tracing and colouring it.

Circle the boys in the below picture.

Tick the objects that Ava should keep in her bag.

Spot 5 differences.

It's matching time! Match the halves with their whole fruit.

Draw lines along the path of the rocket without touching its edges.

Match each sea animal to its correct shadow.

Circle Bella. She has two ponytails. She is wearing a yellow top and carrying a green suitcase.

Tick the thing that Joey can eat.

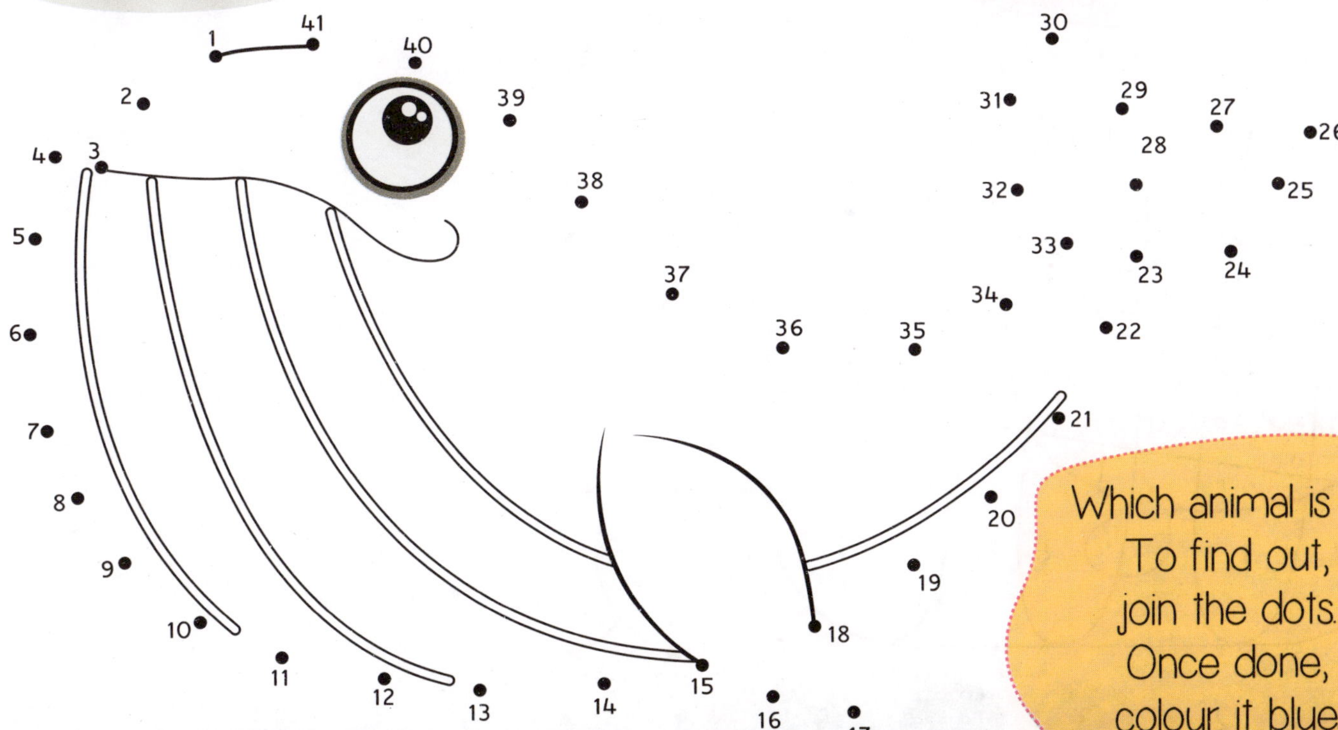

Which animal is it? To find out, join the dots. Once done, colour it blue.

Circle the pair of balls that look alike.

Colour the baby dino according to the colours assigned to each number.

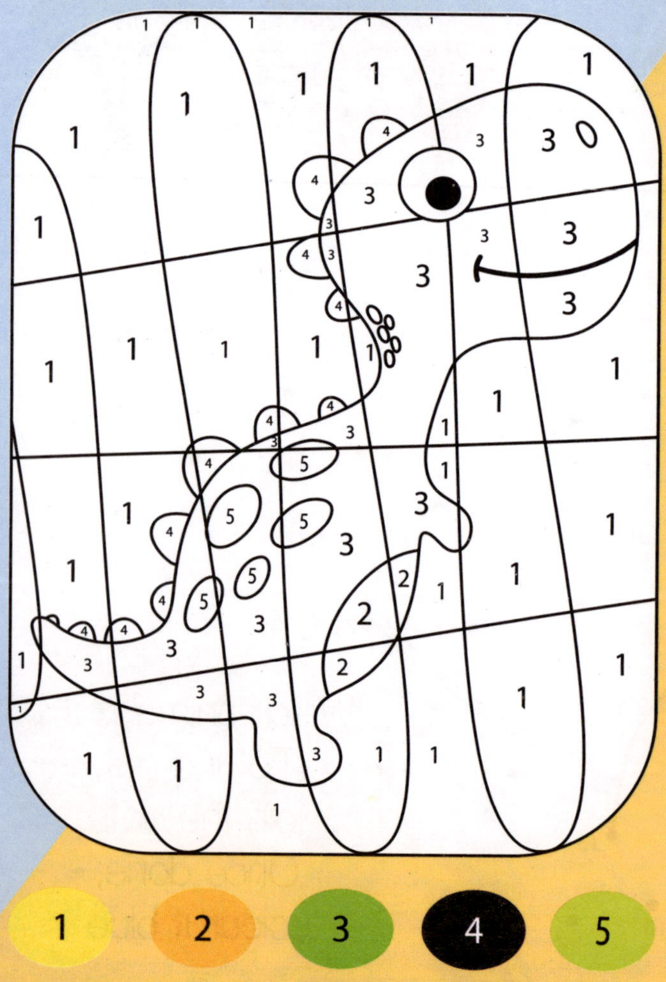

How well can you join the dots? Show us.

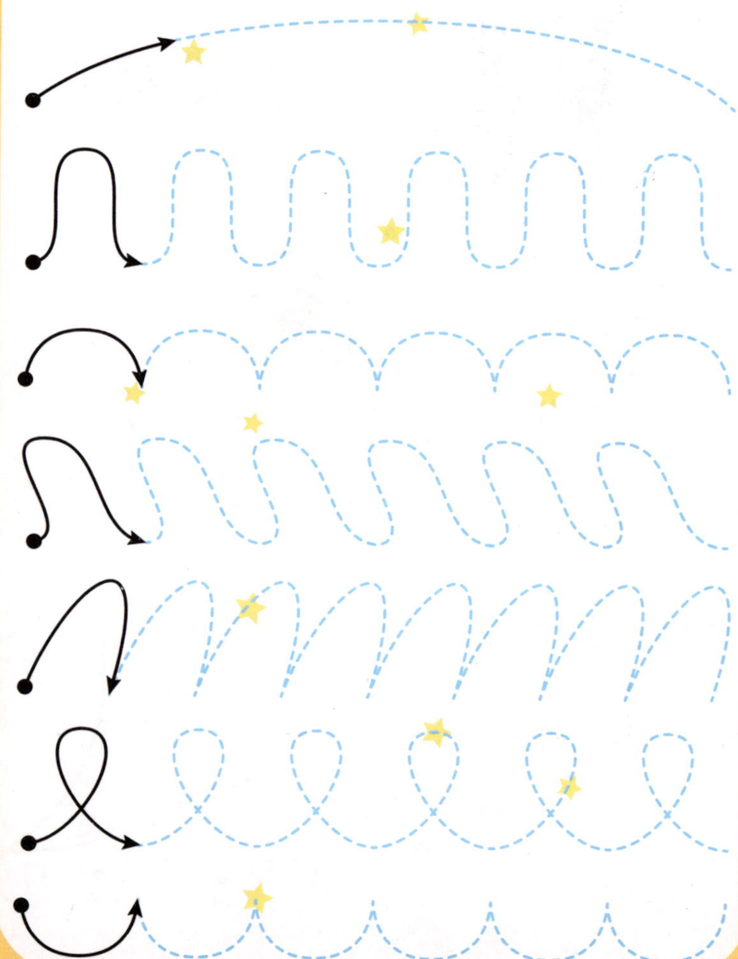

Start from 1 and continue joining the dots till 32 to find out what the picture is.

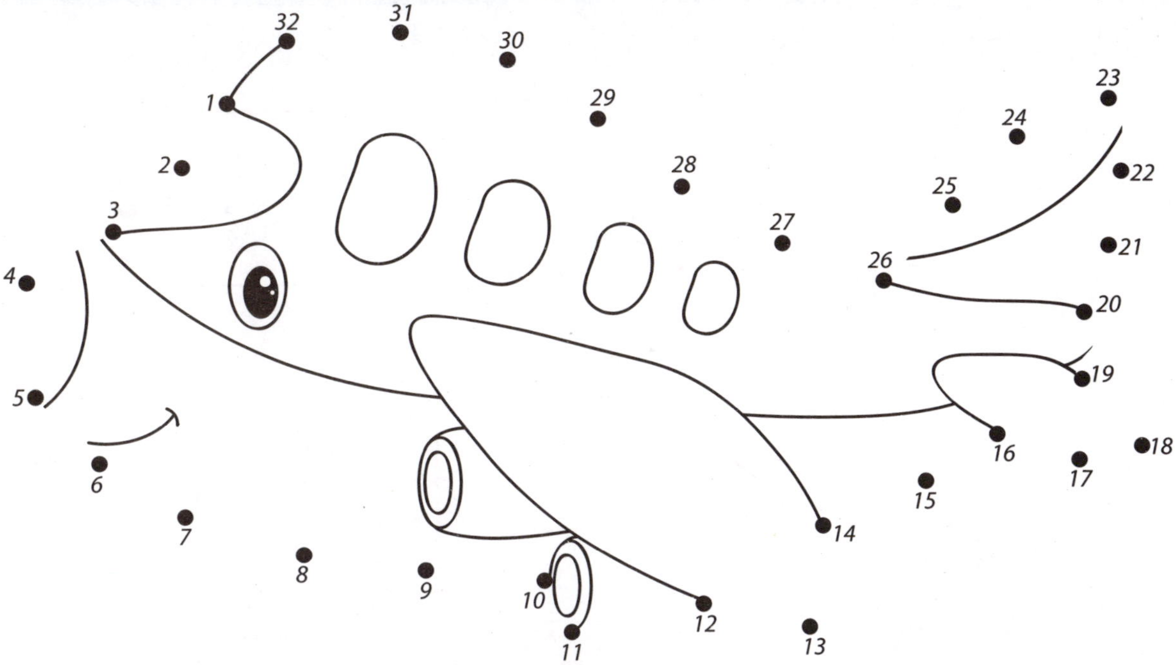

Match each animal with its correct shadow.

Spot 5 differences.

Make the correct pair by colour. Match the gloves to the same coloured caps.

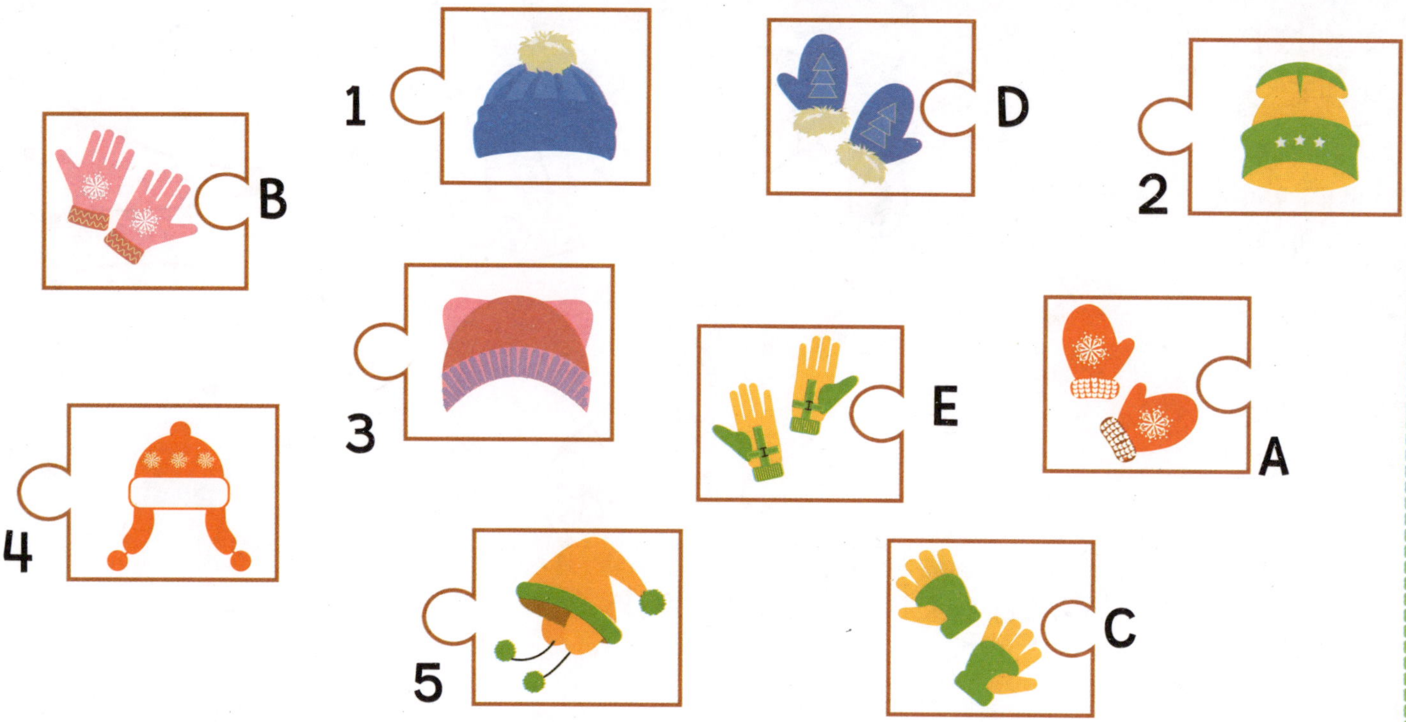

How many ladybugs can you see in the below picture? Write the number in the circle.

Tick the vehicles that do not belong in the air.

Look at all these animal friends riding on a train.
Tick the wagon that has 4 animals in it.

Help each ant reach its leaf by joining the dashed lines.

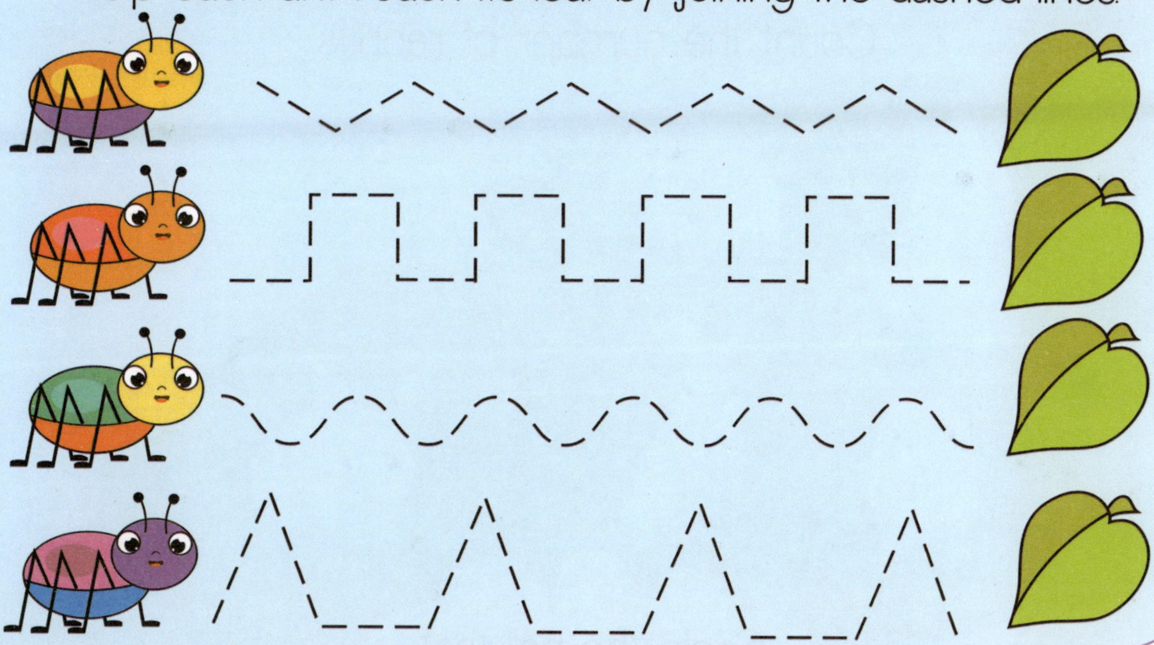

Let's help Tony and Kim find their way to the ice-cream cart.

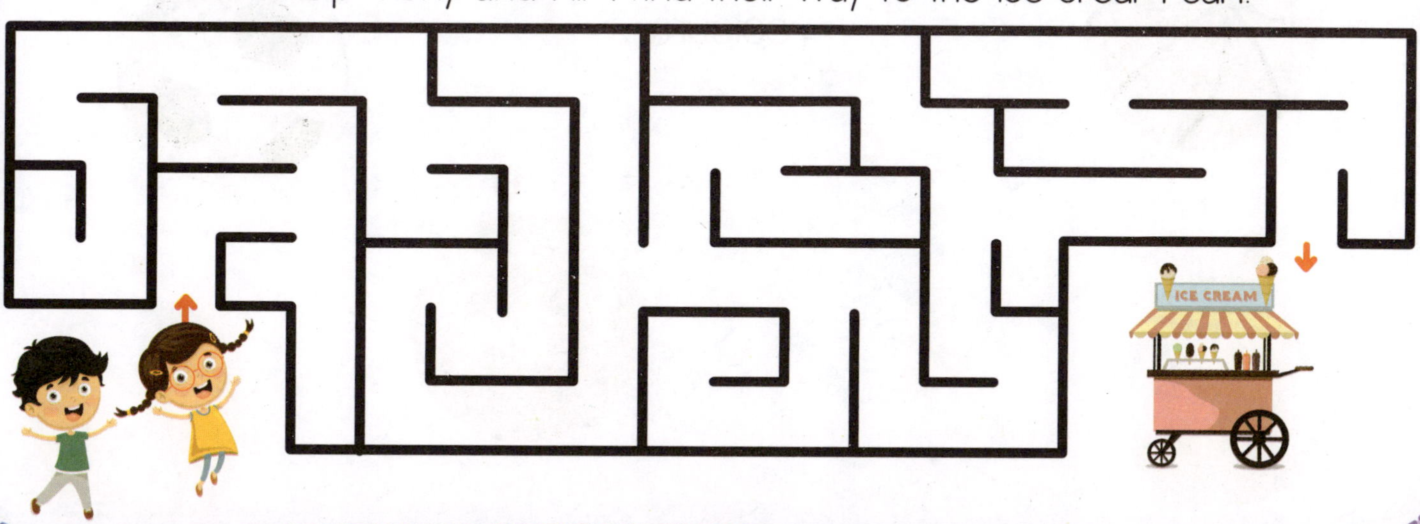

Match the number of candies in each column to their correct number.

A  6

D  8

B  3

E  5

C  2

F  7

Count the number of rabbits.

Circle the ball that has more than 2 colours.

A 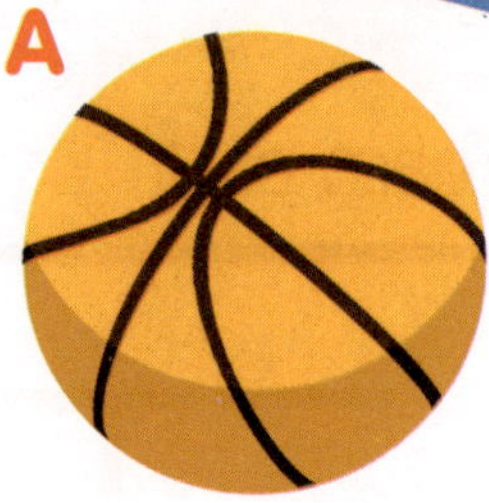

B 

C 

D 

E 

F 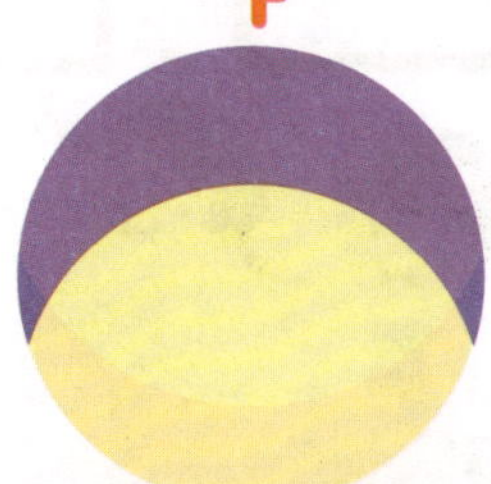

Connect the dots and you'll see a snowman.

Let's colour the truck according to the colours given to each number.

Match each profession to the correct transport.

Match each kid to his/her shadow.

Count the pieces of each shape and write down their numbers.

How does a plant grow? Write 1, 2, 3, 4, 5 and 6 in the correct order.

Can you find Christina? She is wearing two yellow clips in her hair.

Write down the numbers of turtle, jellyfish, starfish and octopus that you can see in the picture.

Turtle: ______ **Jellyfish:** ______ **Starfish:** ______ **Octopus:** ______

Circle the monsters that have the same colour.

Which popsicle looks like a slice of watermelon? Circle it.

Which room is it? Tick the answer.

Bathroom ☐ **Kitchen** ☐ **Drawing Room** ☐ **Bedroom** ☐

Count the number of animals and birds. Write your answers.

Animals: ________

Birds: ________

Help the king of the jungle to reach the forest.

Match the activity with the correct picture.

listening to music **singing** **playing guitar**

Write the missing numbers.

Circle all the red fruits in the picture.

It is said, "books are one's best friend!" Count and write the total number of books in the below picture.

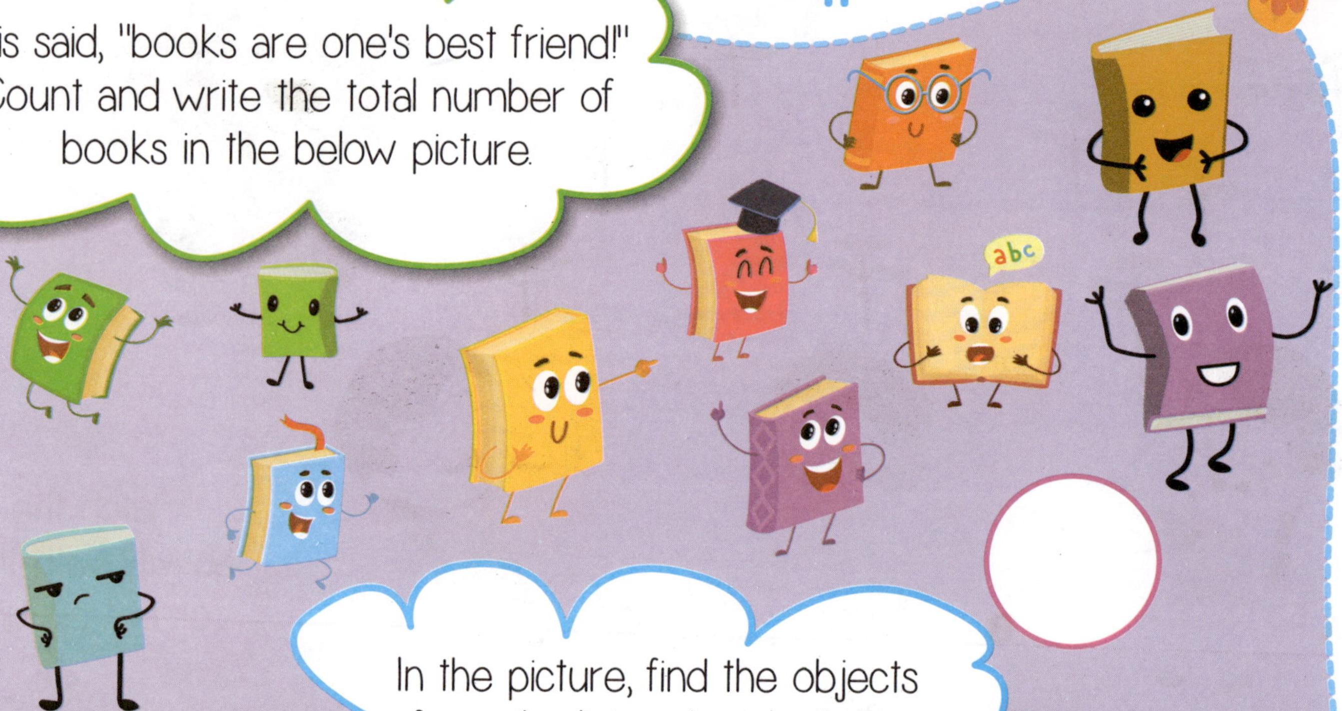

In the picture, find the objects from the list and circle them.

Pillow

Table Lamp

Toy train

Teddybear

What is the best way to use the kitchen? Help Ross find out the steps in the correct order by writing 1, 2 and 3 on each picture.

My name is Carrie and this is my family. My family and I are going on a trip. Match the correct number to show who is who?

1. Me
2. My brother
3. My mother
4. My grandfather
5. My father
6. My grandmother

Can you spot Tia? She is running behind the butterfly and is holding a net in her hand.

Tick the correct way to ride a bicycle.

A

B

A

B

Tick the correct way to cross the road.

Tick the pair of kids who show the right way of eating ice cream.

A

B

Write 1, 2, 3 and 4 on the pictures in the order you should do things after you wake up.

Colour the elephant.

Count and write the number of lamp posts in the below picture.

Find and circle.

3 butterflies 1 windmill A basket full of apples A rabbit A boy

Penny doesn't know the name of the season. Look at her clothes and help her find out what season it is.

- Winter Season
- Rainy Season
- Summer Season

Which one is the correct way to eat your breakfast?

A

B

Look at the below image and tick on what it is called

Bedroom   Living room   Kitchen   Bathroom

Find and circle Edward! He is wearing glasses and is writing in his notebook.

Count the number of starfish and shells in the below picture.

Tick the vehicles that you can see on land

Look at the image and tick on what it is called

Bedroom

Living room

Kitchen

Bathroom

Spot at least 5 differences.

Look at the objects below and guess what season it is.

Tick the odd one out.

Tick the correct way to make Earth a better place to live.

James wants to help his mother in the kitchen. Help him find the vegetables.

Count the number of toes you have on one foot and the number of fingers in your one hand.

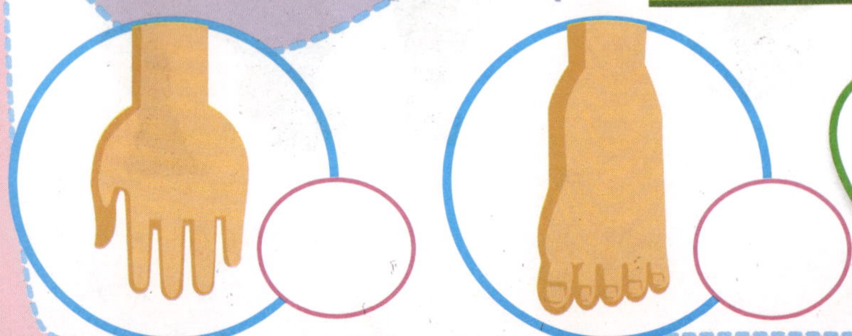

Tick the pictures that start with letter A.

1

2

3

4

Edward loves to paint. Name the object that he has painted.

Do you have flowers at your home? Draw the other half of this flower.

Draw a circle around the odd one out in each row.

The mouse is hungry. Count and write the pieces of cheese that you can feed it.

Should Elena play with her friends at night?

Yes

No

Tick the odd one out.

Spot at least 5 differences.

Circle the duck going in the opposite direction.

Tick the pictures that start with letter B.

Which of the following can you use to clean your room?

Count and write.

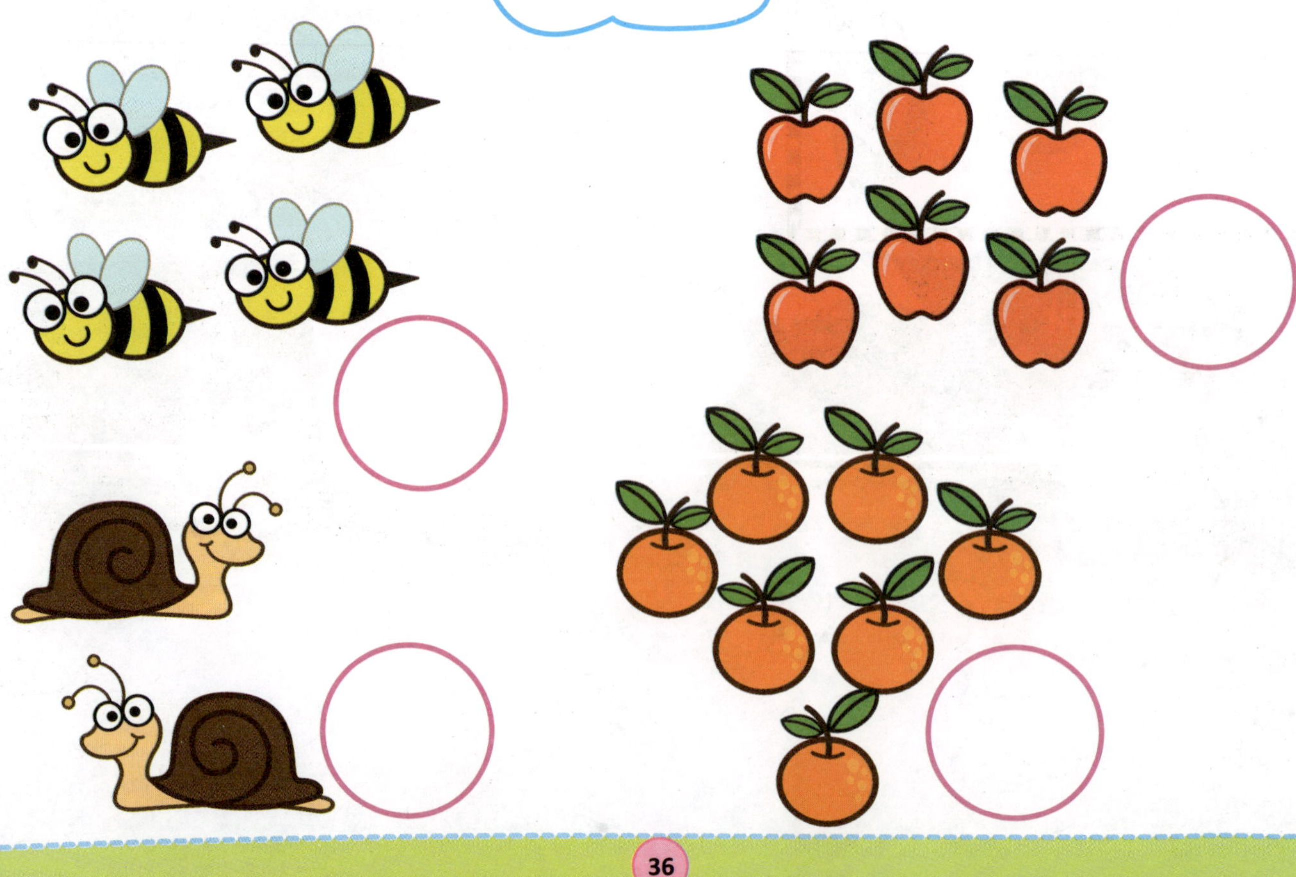

Find and circle the objects given on the right.

Stairs **Mirror** **Door**

Find and tick the things as given at the top of the picture.

Tick the objects that start with letter C.

1

2

3

4

5

Tick the animals that can be a pet.

1

2

3

4

5

6

Match the correct word to its image.

A

B

summer | rainy | winter | spring

C

D

Match the popsicles that are in both the boxes.

Do you know on which planet we live? If yes, circle its picture.

Look at the image and tick on what it is called.

Bedroom

Living room

Kitchen

Bathroom

Circle the bear and the deer in the below picture.

Colour the eggs with as many colours as you like.

Match the following.

Help the cubs find their daddy.
Trace the path with a crayon.

Count the number of flowers and mushrooms that you can see.

Circle the person who treats you when you are sick.

Tick the objects that start with letter F.

Circle the two pairs of cars that share the same colour.

Tick the things that should not be in a bedroom.

Write down if the kids are showing a 'good habit' or a 'bad habit'.

What do you say if someone helps you? Circle your answer.

SORRY

THANK YOU

Tick the things you can see in your bathroom.

Circle the objects that are kept in the kitchen.

Jenny is happy to see so many leaves falling from the trees. Can you guess and write the season?

Amy makes her bed daily in the morning. Is it a good habit?

Spot at least 5 differences.

Match the correct pairs with each other.

 1 a 

 2 b 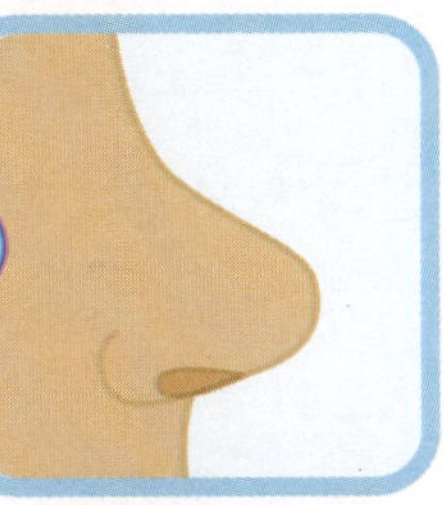

 3 c 

 4 d 

Complete the picture of the sun to make it shine.

Emily and Chris are on vacation.
Can you guess the place by looking at the picture?

Forest

Beach

Park

Tick the objects that do NOT start with letter H.

In the picture below, there are parents in the left column and young ones in the right column. Match the parents to their correct young ones.

Find Jim. He has black curly hair and has a green tube around him.

Two girls are playing with building blocks.
Tick the right way to play.

Rick's family is going on a trip. Can you circle the pet dog in the below picture?

Circle the odd one out.

Tick the activity where you need to use your mouth.

a

b

Count the number of ducklings in the below picture.

Little Ron always keeps his room neat and clean. Is this a good or a bad habit? Tick it.

GOOD **BAD**

Tick at the correct way to treat trees.

A

B

Colour the objects that start with letter J.

Let's match each person to the transport that they use.

1 2 3 4

a b c d

Tick the odd one out in each row.

Tick the things that you can see in a living room.

Mason is going for a winter vacation. Let's help him pack his bag by choosing the correct objects.

Draw the correct shape marked in the circles and draw them in correct missing puzzle pieces.

Tick the objects whose names start with letter K.

Match the objects with the shapes they remind you of.

Look at the picture and circle everything that is green in colour.

Circle the chickens that are facing towards the left direction.

Tick the activity of watching time.

A

B

Colour all the pet animals.

1

2

3

4

5

6

Tick the correct habit.

A

B

Count the different fruits and write their numbers.

 ________

 ________

 ________

Match each animal to its shadow.

Join the dots and complete the picture.

The little puppy wants to go to his kennel. Help him find the way.

Tick the animals that eat grass.

Tick the objects that do not start with letter M.

Spot 5 differences between the two pictures of the vehicles.

Pick the odd one out in each row.

Circle the exactly same looking fruits.

Make your hot air balloon the most beautiful one in the town by colouring it with different colours.

Circle the food items that have the word 'nut' in them.

Tick the odd one out.

Find and circle.

The doll with pink hair.

The chimney of the train.

Tick the vegetables that are used in salads.

Circle all the marine animals.

Spot at least 5 differences between the two pictures.

Tick the things that do not start with letter O.

1

2

3

4

Spot the rabbit in the below picture.

Match the animals with their food in order to feed them.

Tick the things that you will carry during the rainy season.

Tick the birds whose names start with letter P.

Find a broom and candle in the below picture.

Tick the correct way of entering a room.

A

B

Find Sophia and Jayden.

Jayden is wearing blue shorts.
Sophia is hanging upside down.

Pick the odd one out.

Draw lines between the pair of fish that look exactly the same.

'Q is for queen'. Colour this picture of the queen.

Tick the object that is lighter in weight.

Let's do a memory test, shall we?

Count and write the number of the objects asked at the bottom.

Tick the objects that start with letter R.

Tick the odd one out in each row.

Count and write the number of each item.

Butterfly: ________ **Flower:** __________

Name each activity.

Spot and tick the animal playing the guitar.

Tick the odd one out.

'S is for snowman'. Michael has made a snowman. Let's fill colours in it.

Join the dots.

Match the birds with their houses.

1 2 3 4 5 6

A B C D E F

Tick the activity that you need to do in order to take care of your teeth.

Tick the object from which you should drink water.

'H is for helicopter.' Let's colour the helicopter.

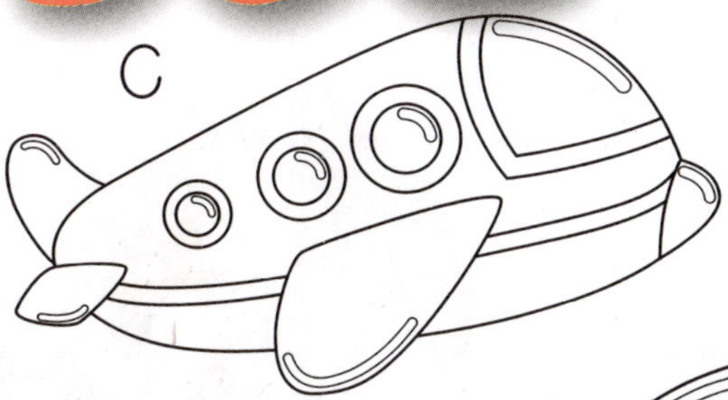

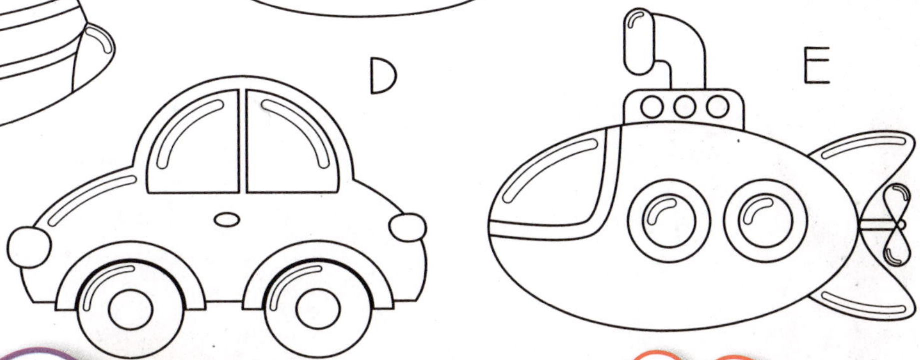

Match the objects with their cases.

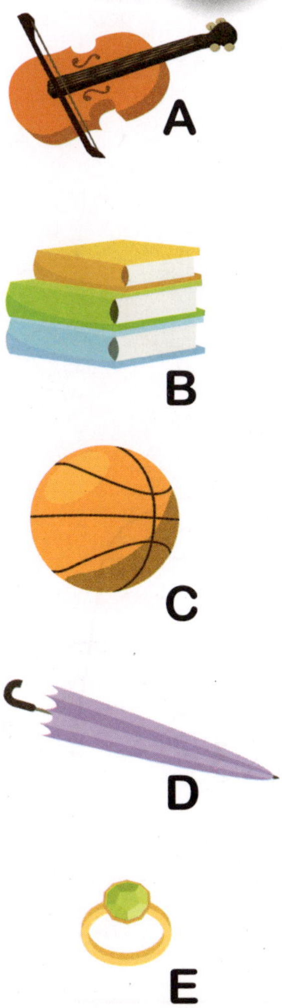

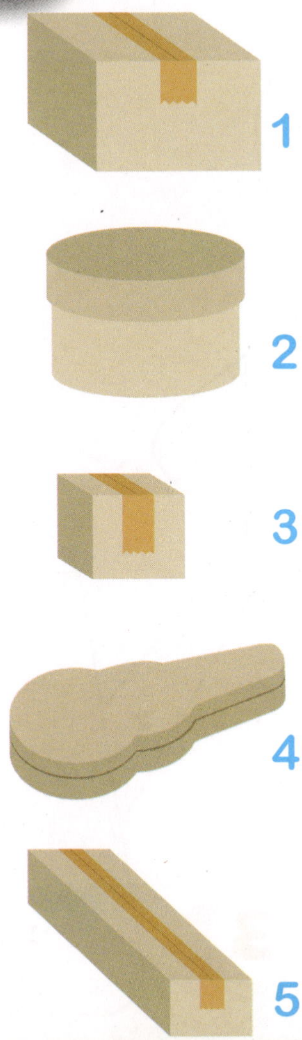

Tick the odd one out.

Can you spot a starfish, a yellow flower and red berries? If yes, circle them.

Colour by numbers.

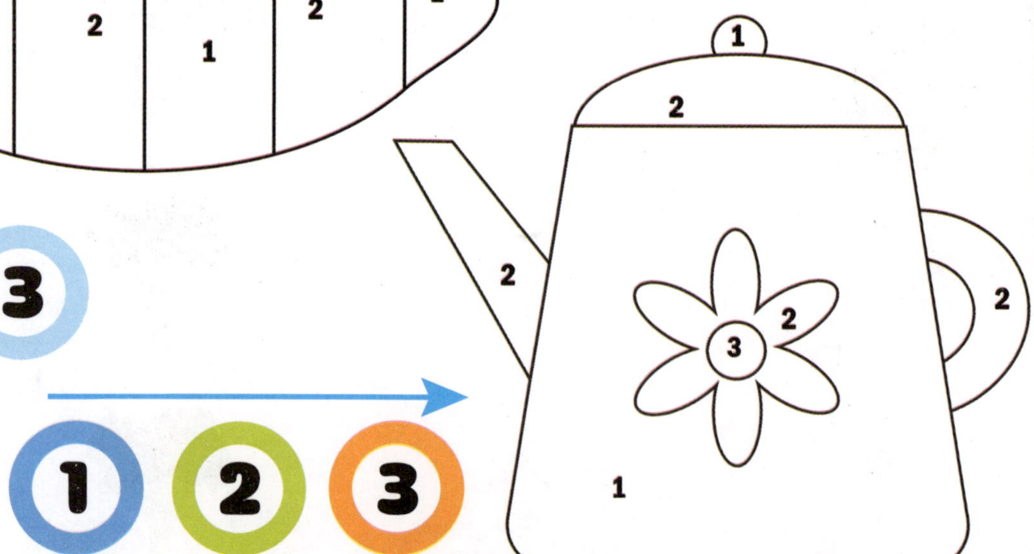

Let's join the dots!

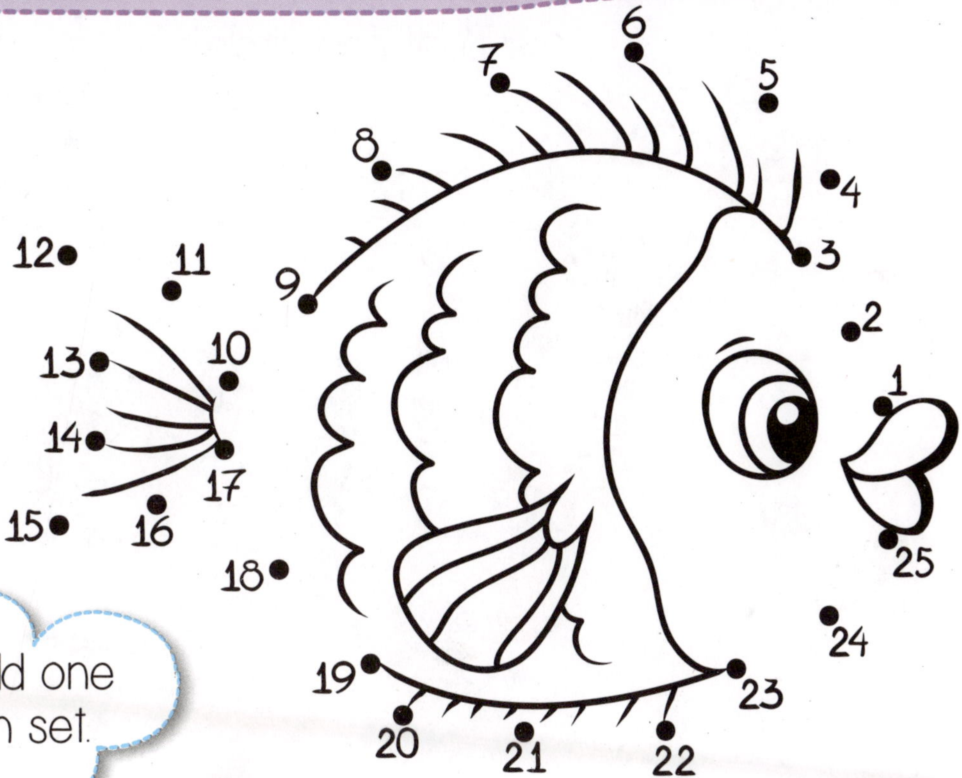

Tick the odd one out in each set.

Circle the vehicle that can go to the moon.

Spot and circle!

- Find Mark, he is riding a bicycle.
- Find Henry, he is playing with sand.
- Find Tia, she is riding a scooter.

Match the following to maintain proper hygiene of the different body parts.

A

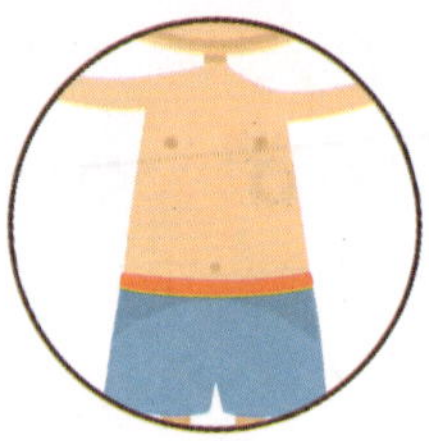

B

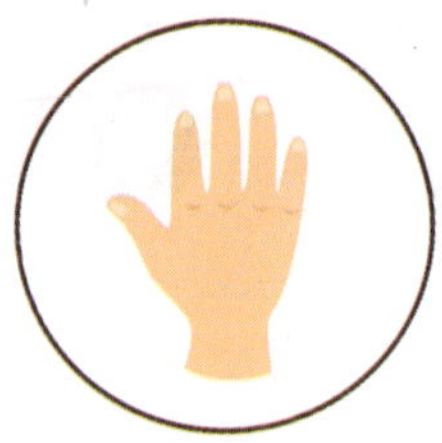

C

D

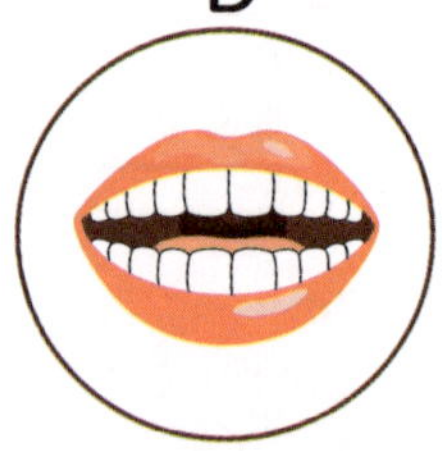

1

2

3

4

Which one is the correct time to wake up?

A

B

Count the objects in the tree and write their quantity.

Which of them is smaller?

Circle the tube that is showing the sign of 'thumbs up'.

Circle the uppercase letters.

a b c d e F g

H i j k L m n o

p Q r s t U

v w x Y z

Tick the objects that start with letter Y.

Count and write.

Butterflies: --------

Bees: --------

Ladybugs: --------

A. Jenny: the woman reading a story from the book

B. Paul: Looking closely at the butterfly

C. Canvas, with a painting on it

Complete the rocket by drawing and colouring on its other half.

'Z is for zebra'. Colour the stripes of the zebra in black.

Who is winning the race? Write 1, 2 or 3 next to each animal to show their positions.

Complete the series.

A ___ C ___ E ___ G

Tick the faster vehicle.

Circle the biggest fruit.

Draw a circle around the pencil in the middle.

Tick the object you need to clean your teeth.

Match the animals with the letters they start with.

1 2 3 4

B	C	D	E
A	B	C	D

Complete the series.

1 ___ 3 ___ 5 ___

Count and write the number of:

Tick the body part we use to walk.

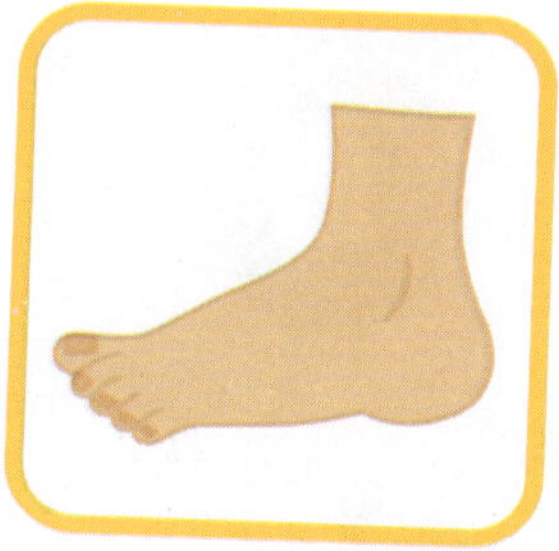

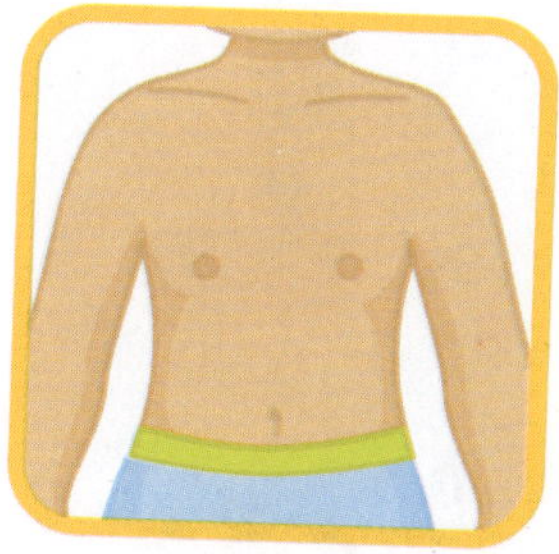

Circle the owl that is purple in colour.

Draw a circle around the smallest sandwich.

Match each animal to the first letter of its name.

L P O K

Circle the crayon on the left of the red one.

Tick the correct shadow of the tiger.

It's colour time. Let's match the words to the colours!

ORANGE

YELLOW

GREEN

BLUE

PINK

RED

Circle the smaller one in each pair.

Match each picture with its shadow.

Colour the snail and the leaf using the colour codes. Have fun!

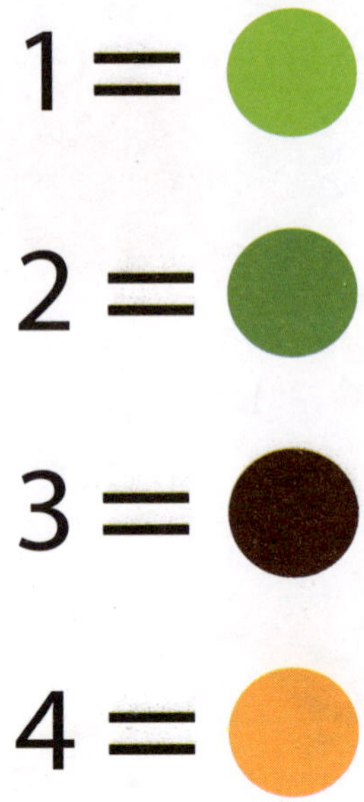

Can you help mother hen to count her eggs? Write your answer in the box.

The monkey loves to eat bananas. Help him to get some.

Match the sea animals to their missing parts.

Can you find the right animal whose part is given in the left row? Tick them.

1

A

B

C

2

A

B

C

3

A

B

C

4

A

B

C

ANSWERS

Page-3
Tick: goat, cow, sheep and horse.
Write numbers in the circles: 1-wake up, 2-toilet, 3-brushing teeth, 4-take a bath, 5-eat breakfast.
Draw lines: happy-3 ; sad-1 confused-2; and surprised-4.

Page-4

Draw lines to match: hand-gloves, foot-shoes, and head-hat.
Banana and mango to be coloured yellow.

Page-5
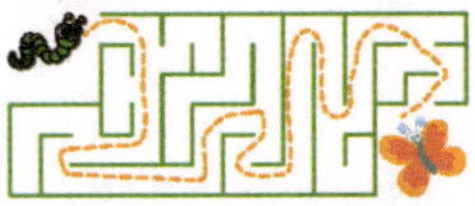
Duckling: Tick 2.
Stars: Circle all the stars.

Page-6
Circle the two birds.
Bear: Join the dashed lines.
Find and circle: Circle the 3 rabbits and 3 foxes.

Page-7

Match: 1-D, 2-C, 3-A, 4-E and 5-B.
Tick: the cow.

Page-8

Draw lines: A - 5, B - 3, C - 1, D - 2 AND E - 4.
Colour: Strawberry, cherries and apple to be coloured red.

Page-9

Birds: Write 'No' in the circle.

Page-10
Order the activities like this: 3, 1, 2.
Ladybug: 1-B, 2-C, 3-D and 4-A.

Page-11
Circle the boys: First, Third and Fifth.

Page-12
Draw lines: 1-E, 2-D, 3-A, 4-B and 5-C.
Match: 1-C, 2-D, 3-A, 4-E and 5-B.

Page-13
Circle Bella: The girl on the first right.
Joey: Tick the apple.

Page-14

Colour: 1-yellow, 2-orange, 3-green, 4-black and 5-light green.
Trace all the lines.

Page-15

Match picture with shadow: A-3, B-4, C-1 and D-2.

Page-16
Draw lines to match: A-4, B-3, C-5, D-1 and E-2.
Bugs: Write 10 in the circle.
Vehicle: Tick the cycle, fire-engine, police car, scooter, taxi and boat.

Page-17
Tick the last wagon.
Lines: Join the dashed lines.
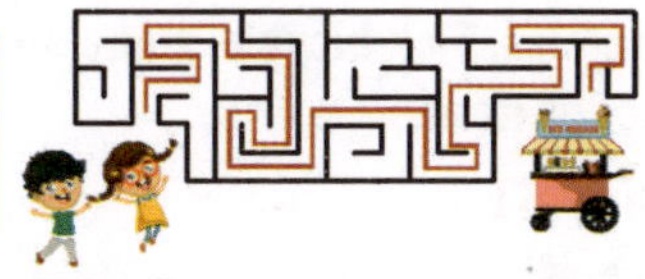

Page-18
Match: A-2, B-6, C-3, D-5, E-7 and F-8.
Count the rabbits: Write 10 in the circle.
Ball: Circle B.

Page-19
Colour the truck by numbers.
Match: 1-D, 2-C, 3-A and 4-B.

Page-20
Match: A-3, B-1, C-2, D-5 and E-4.
Square: 8, Circle: 9, Star: 7, Triangle: 7, Heart: 6
Plant growth: Write the numbers in this order: 4, 2, 6, 1, 3, 5

Page-21
Christina: B.
Count: Turtle- 2, Jellyfish- 2, Starfish- 2, Octopus- 1
Circle: 3 and 5 (the two green monsters)

Page-22
Popsicle: Circle 5
Tick: Bedroom
Count: Animals- 6 and Birds-5.

Page-23

Match- A-playing guitar, B- listening to music and C-singing.

Page-24
Circle: 1, 2, 3, 10 and 11.
Count: Write 11 in the circle.

Page-25
Steps: Write 3, 2 and 1 in respective circles.
Carrie's family: Match A-2, B-6, C-5, D-1, E-4 and F-3.
Spot Tia: the running girl

Page-26
Bicycle: Tick B.
Road cross: Tick A.
Habit: Tick A.

Page-27
Things to do: 3, 4, 1, 2
Colour: Colour the elephant.
Count and write : 7

Page-28

Season: Tick Rainy Season.
Breakfast: Tick A.

Page-29

Tick: Living room.

Page-30

Count: Starfish- 2, Shells- 3

Vehicles: Tick bicycle, ambulance, cargo truck, car and school bus.

Tick: Kitchen.

Page-31

Guess season: Write 'Summer'

Odd one: Tick on gorilla.

Page-32

Tick: A.

Count: Write 5 in each circle.

Page-33

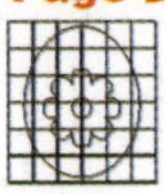

Tick: 1-apple, 2-alligator and 4-airplane.

Name the object: Write 'Tree'.

Page-34

Cheese: Write 7.

Play: Tick 'No'.

Page-35

Page-36

Tick 1-butterfly, 3-broccoli and 5-ball.

Count & Write: bees-4, snails-2, apples-6 and oranges-7.

Page-37

Page-38

Tick 1-camel, 3-cactus and 4-cow.

Pet: Tick 1-cat, 2-dog, 4- fish and 6-rabbit.

Seasons: Summer: B, Rainy: D, Winter: C and Spring: A.

Page-39

Circle: Earth.

Tick: Bathroom.

Page-40

Colour all the three Eggs.

Match: A-4, B-1, C-5, D-2 and E-3.

Page-41

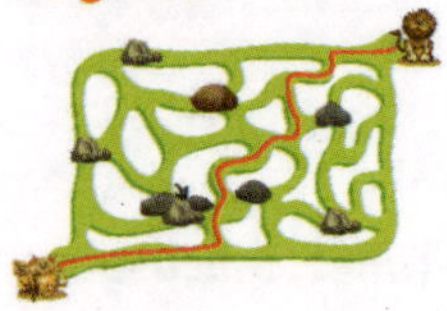

Count: Flowers-10 and mushrooms-4.

Page-42

Tick: C- doctor.

Tick 1-football, 3-flower and 5-fire.

Page-43

Habit: Write 'Good habit'.

Circle: Thank you.

Page-44

Bathroom: Tick 2-toothpaste, 3-soap, 4-toothbrush, 5-towel and 9-sponge.

Kitchen: Circle 1-vessel, 3-peeler, 4-pan and 6-peas.

Season: Write Autumn.

Page-45

Habit: Tick 'Yes'.

Match: 1-d, 2-c, 3-b and 4-a.

Page-46

Guess the place: Tick Beach.

Tick: 1-popsicle, 2-fish and 5-truck.

Page-47

Match: a-4, b-1, c-2 and d-3.

Find Jim: Circle 1.

Page-48

Tick: B

Odd one: Circle b-ice-cream cone.

Page-49

Mouth: Tick a-girl eating ice-cream.

Ducklings: Write 8 in the circle.

Ron: Tick 'Good'.

Page-50

Tick: B-man watering plants.

J: Colour the jar and the jellyfish.

Match: 1-d; 2-b; 3-a; 4-c.

Page-51

Tick: 1-sofa, 2-coffee table and 5-lamp.

Circle: 2-cap, 6-sweater and 7-gloves.

Page-52

Match: 1- star; 2- square; 3- circle; 4- triangle.

Tick: 1-kettle, 2-key and 5-kite.

Shadow: Match 1-e, 2-d, 3-a, 4-c and 5-b.

Page-53

Page-54
Tick: B
Colour: 1-puppy, 3-kitten and 4-fish.

Page-55
Tick: B-Picture of the boy throwing litter in the dustbin.
Count: Write pear-8, pineapple-7, apple-10.
Match the shadows: 1-c, 2-b, 3-d, 4-e and 5-a.

Page-56

Animals that eat grass: 1-cow, 2-goat and 6-sheep.

Page-57
Tick: 2-orange, 3-ladybug and 5-apple.

Page-58

Colour the hot air balloon in different colours.
Circle: 1-cashews, 2-groundnuts and 5-coconut.

Page-59

Tick: 1-broccoli, 2-cucumber, 3-carrot, 4-tomatoes and 5-beetroot.

Page-60

Tick: 1-apple and 3-cargo van.

Page-61

Match: 1-e, 2-c, 3-b, 4-a and 5-d.
Rain: 1-umbrella, 4-raincoat and 8-gumboots.

Page-62

Birds: Tick 1-pigeon and 6-parrot.

Page-63
Room: Tick B- boy knocking at the door before entering.

Page-64
Identical: Draw a line connecting C and N fish.
Colour the queen.
Tick the feather.

Page-65
Memory test: Write dice-5, boots-3, car-4, cherry-2, strawberry-4 and umbrella-3.

Page-66
Count: Write butterfly-6 and flower-6.
Write the Activities: 1-basketball, 2-football, 3-cycling, 4-skipping rope and 5-skating.
Tick hippopotamus.

Page-67
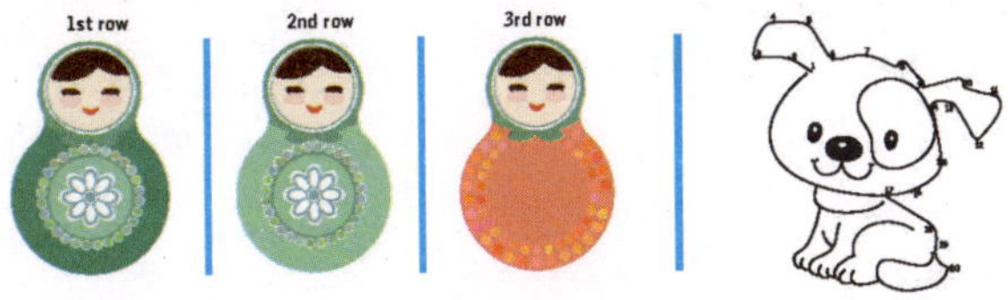

Colour the snowman.

Page-68
Match: 1-B; 2-F; 3-E; 4-C; 5-A; 6-D
Tick the image of boy brushing teeth.

Page-69
Colour: B.
Match: A-4, B-1, C-2, D-5 and E-3.

Page-70

Colour: Honey bee: 1-black, 2-yellow, 3-light blue.
kettle: 1-blue, 2-light green, 3-orange.

Page-71
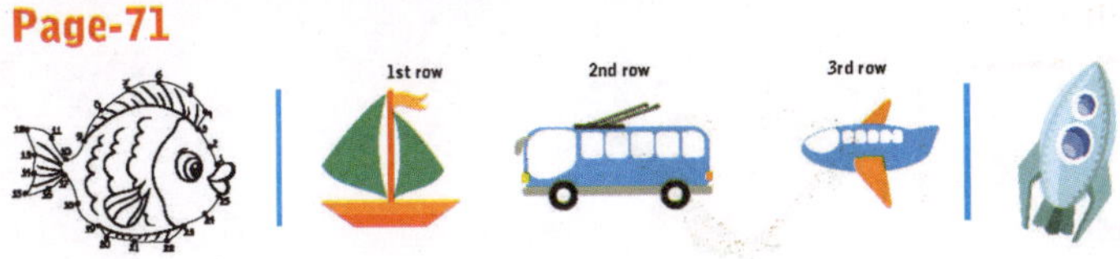

Page-72

Match: A-2, B-4, C-1 and D-3.
Tick: A.

Page-73

Smaller: rabbit
Circle the blue tube.

Page-74

Circle F, H, L, Q, S, U, W and Y.
Count: Write butterflies-3, bees-4 and ladybugs-1.
Circle: 1-yak, 2-yam, 5-yacht and 6-yo-yo.

Page-75

Colour zebra in black and white.
Complete colouring the rocket.

Page-76

Complete the series: B, D, F.
Tick bike.

Page-77

Circle: Yellow pencil.

Page-78

Match: 1-A, 2-D, 3-B, 4-C
Complete the series: Write 2, 4 and 6 respectively.

Page-79

Purple Owl: Circle owl in the middle.

Page-80

Match L-2, P-1, O-4 and K-3.
Circle: the yellow crayon.
Shadow: Tick B.

Page-81

Shadows: 1-Octopus, 2-Angel Fish, 3-Dolphin, 4-Seahorse, 5- Clownfish and 6-Crab.

Page-82

Colour the snail using: 1-light green, 2-dark green, 3-brown and 5-orange.
Count Eggs: Write 12.

Page-83

Match: 1-e, 2-a, 3-c, 4-d, 5-f and 6-b.

Page-84

Match: 1-B, 2-C, 3-A and 4-C.